IT'S TIME TO EAT JUJUBE

It's Time to Eat JUJUBE

Walter the Educator

Silent King Books
A WhichHead Entertainment Imprint

Copyright © 2024 by Walter the Educator

All rights reserved. No part of this book may be reproduced in any manner whatsoever without written per- mission except in the case of brief quotations embodied in critical articles and reviews.

First Printing, 2024

Disclaimer

This book is a literary work; the story is not about specific persons, locations, situations, and/or circumstances unless mentioned in a historical context. Any resemblance to real persons, locations, situations, and/or circumstances is coincidental. This book is for entertainment and informational purposes only. The author and publisher offer this information without warranties expressed or implied. No matter the grounds, neither the author nor the publisher will be accountable for any losses, injuries, or other damages caused by the reader's use of this book. The use of this book acknowledges an understanding and acceptance of this disclaimer.

It's Time to Eat JUJUBE is a collectible early learning book by Walter the Educator suitable for all ages belonging to Walter the Educator's Time to Eat Book Series. Collect more books at WaltertheEducator.com

USE THE EXTRA SPACE TO TAKE NOTES AND DOCUMENT YOUR MEMORIES

JUJUBE

It's time to eat, oh what a treat,

It's Time to Eat

Jujube

A jujube snack is hard to beat!

So small and round, like little jewels,

A fruit so sweet, it follows no rules.

Its skin is smooth, a shiny red,

A yummy bite to keep you fed.

Crunchy fresh or dried and chewy,

Jujubes are tasty, soft, and gooey.

Pick them fresh right from the tree,

Or grab a bowl and snack with glee.

The flavor's mild, a little sweet,

A perfect fruit for hands and feet!

Slice them up or eat them whole,

Jujubes make your tummy feel full.

Packed with goodness, vitamins too,

A healthy snack for me and you.

It's Time to Eat

Jujube

In the sunshine, they love to grow,

A gift from nature's garden show.

From far-off lands, they've come to stay,

To make our snacking bright today.

Some say they taste like dates or figs,

Little fruits that give you big digs.

Take a bite, you'll surely smile,

Jujubes make life so worthwhile.

Make some tea or cook them in stew,

Jujubes bring flavor in all that you do.

A fruit so small, yet full of power,

It's nature's gem, a snack to devour.

Share them with friends or save a few,

Jujubes are perfect to enjoy with you.

Pack them in lunches, take them to play,

It's Time to Eat

Jujube

A fruit that's fun all through the day!

So shout hooray, let's take a bite,

Jujubes make the moment just right.

Crunchy, chewy, red, or brown,

The best little snack around the town.

And don't forget, when seeds you see,

Plant them deep, and grow a tree!

Jujubes will grow and thrive,

It's Time to Eat
Jujube

A fruity friend that comes alive!

ABOUT THE CREATOR

Walter the Educator is one of the pseudonyms for Walter Anderson. Formally educated in Chemistry, Business, and Education, he is an educator, an author, a diverse entrepreneur, and he is the son of a disabled war veteran.
"Walter the Educator" shares his time between educating and creating. He holds interests and owns several creative projects that entertain, enlighten, enhance, and educate, hoping to inspire and motivate you. Follow, find new works, and stay up to date with Walter the Educator™
at WaltertheEducator.com

www.ingramcontent.com/pod-product-compliance
Lightning Source LLC
LaVergne TN
LVHW052013060526
838201LV00059B/4002